America at WAR

WORLD WAR II
TEN GREATEST HEROES

John Perritano

Created by Q2AMedia

www.q2amedia.com

Text, design & illustrations Copyright © Q2AMedia 2011

Editor Jessica Cohn
Project Manager Shekhar Kapur
Art Director Joita Das
Designers Isha Khanna and Deepika Verma
Picture Researchers Akansha Srivastava and Nivisha Sinha

10 9 8 7 6 5 4 3 2 1

ISBN10: 93-810870-2-4
ISBN13: 978-9-381-08702-2

Printed in China

Contents

World at War   4

- James H. Doolittle   6
- Chester W. Nimitz   8
- John Basilone   10
- Georgi Zhukov   12
- George S. Patton   14
- Tommy Macpherson   16
- Audie Murphy   18
- Anthony McAuliffe   20
- Henry Mucci   22
- Daniel Inouye   24

Hall of Heroes   26

Heroes of the Holocaust   28

Glossary/Index   32

World at War

December 7, 1941, was a typical Sunday at Pearl Harbor, Hawaii, home of the U.S. Pacific Fleet. Many servicemen and women were dressing for worship services. Others were crowding mess halls to eat breakfast. Those on duty worked aboard warships in the harbor.

On December 29, 1940, London was firebombed by the Germans.

Just before dawn, 33 Japanese warships, including six aircraft carriers, had cruised within 200 miles of the island of Oahu in Hawaii. Their mission was to surprise the Americans and to destroy the fleet. At 7:55 a.m., the first wave of Japanese planes attacked. A second wave later joined the fight. By the time the smoke had cleared, the Japanese had killed more than 2,000 Americans and had sunk or damaged many ships. A day after the attack, the United States declared war on Japan.

U.S. President Franklin Roosevelt declared December 7, 1941, when Pearl Harbor was attacked, "a date that will live in infamy."

In September 1939, the Nazis advanced through Poland.

Nations Aligned

In World War II (WWII), the Axis powers of Germany, Italy, and Japan fought against the Allied nations, led by the United States, the Soviet Union, and Great Britain. The U.S. was a latecomer. The conflict began in 1939, when Nazi Germany invaded Poland. During the next six years, some 60 million people—no one knows the exact number—would die in the war. Most were civilians. No corner of the globe was spared.

Many Heroes

WWII highlighted the worst of human savagery. Yet there were many heroes. Some were military leaders such as General Dwight D. Eisenhower, who commanded the Allied armies in Europe. Others were common soldiers, such as Beauford T. Anderson. In 1945, Anderson killed 25 Japanese soldiers during heavy fighting on the island of Okinawa. Many people outside the military were also heroic, including Giovanni Palatucci, an Italian policeman who risked his life to save thousands of Jews from death.

These are some of their stories.

James H. Doolittle

The attack on Pearl Harbor had heavily damaged the U.S. Navy's Pacific Fleet. In 1942, Imperial Japan controlled the ocean and the air. Its army marched into Malaya, Burma, and the Philippines. By the end of April, most of Southeast Asia was under Japanese control.

The deck of the USS *Hornet* served as a runway for the bombers.

A Daring Feat

The United States desperately needed a victory. U.S. President Franklin D. Roosevelt urged his military leaders to strike back. He called for a daring raid against Japan to even the score for Pearl Harbor. It was a difficult assignment. No plane then built could reach the Japanese islands from U.S. bases. Some believed that medium-range bombers could reach Japan if the planes took off from an aircraft carrier. However, after such a raid, the crews would have to land the planes in China because there would not be enough fuel for the trip home.

James H. Doolittle

Born:	December 14, 1896
Hometown:	Alameda, California
Branch of Service:	U.S. Army Air Corps
Rank:	Lieutenant Colonel
Heroic Moment:	Raid on Japan

Wings of a Hero

Lieutenant Colonel James Doolittle, 45, was an experienced **aviator**. He once flew a fighter plane even though he had two broken ankles. At 8 a.m. on April 18, 1942, Doolittle led 16 B-25 bombers off the deck of the USS *Hornet*. Each plane carried 2,000 pounds of bombs. The Japanese, believing their island nation was safe from attack, panicked when the bombers appeared over Tokyo and several other cities.

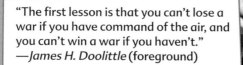

> "The first lesson is that you can't lose a war if you have command of the air, and you can't win a war if you haven't."
> —*James H. Doolittle* (foreground)

Success or Failure?

Doolittle's planes dropped their bombs and sped away. Fifteen planes steered toward China. One made its way to Russia. Some of the crewmen were forced to bail out. Other planes crash-landed in the ocean. All the bombers were lost. Eleven airmen died or were captured. However, most of the 80 crewmembers survived, including Doolittle.

Second Thoughts

Doolittle thought the raid was a failure. The bombs did little damage. He had lost all of his aircraft. He believed the army would **court-martial** him. Instead, the mission boosted morale in the United States. The public hailed Doolittle and his men as heroes. More importantly, the raid caused the Japanese to rethink their strategy in the Pacific. That led to their major defeat during the Battle of Midway two months later. One Japanese official said the Doolittle raid "passed like a shiver over Japan."

Sailors aboard a Navy cruiser watched the B-25 bombers take off for Japan.

Chester W. Nimitz

In June 1942, Japanese Admiral Isoroku Yamamoto, the mastermind behind the attack on Pearl Harbor, took aim at Midway, a tiny island located about 1,000 miles northwest of Hawaii. If the attack succeeded, the Japanese would take over Midway. They would be in a position to cripple the U.S. Navy's Pacific Fleet.

Taking Aim

Yamamoto planned to destroy the island's defenses and force American aircraft carriers out into the open. Capturing Midway would also plug a gap in Japan's defensive forces, which stretched more than 12,000 miles from the Aleutian Islands in Alaska to Singapore in the south. Before Doolittle's daring raid, many Japanese military commanders thought Yamamoto's plan was too risky. After the raid, they feared that Japan was vulnerable to an attack. They came to believe that taking Midway would make their homeland safer.

"Our armament must be adequate to the needs, but our faith is not primarily in these machines of defense, but in ourselves."
—*Chester W. Nimitz*

U.S. oil tanks were set afire during the Japanese air raid on Midway.

Chester W. Nimitz

Born:	February 24, 1885
Hometown:	Kerrville, Texas
Branch of Service:	U.S. Navy
Rank:	Admiral
Heroic Moment:	Battle of Midway

Springing a Trap

Unfortunately for Yamamoto, the Americans had figured out his plans. U.S. Admiral Chester Nimitz, who commanded the U.S. Pacific Fleet, sent a small task force to the Aleutians in case the Japanese decided to attack there. In a brilliant move, he split his main force into two carrier groups. He sent both groups to Midway to surprise Yamamoto. On June 4, 1942, a U.S. Navy plane spotted the enemy approaching the island. The battle was on.

Cunning Fight

Admiral Raymond A. Spruance, the American in command at Midway, ordered his planes into the sky. The American planes bombed the decks of the Japanese aircraft carriers. During the Battle of Midway, aircraft from the Japanese carrier *Hiryu* were able to sink the U.S. carrier *Yorktown*. But by the end of the battle, the Americans had destroyed four Japanese carriers, including the *Hiryu*.

Beaten and Bloody

Admiral Nimitz's cunning and Spruance's boldness forced Yamamoto's fighters back to Japan, beaten and bloody. After Midway, the Japanese navy never regained the upper hand in the Pacific war. The tide had now turned in favor of the U.S.

Admiral Isoroku Yamamoto was eventually shot down when flying in the Solomon Islands.

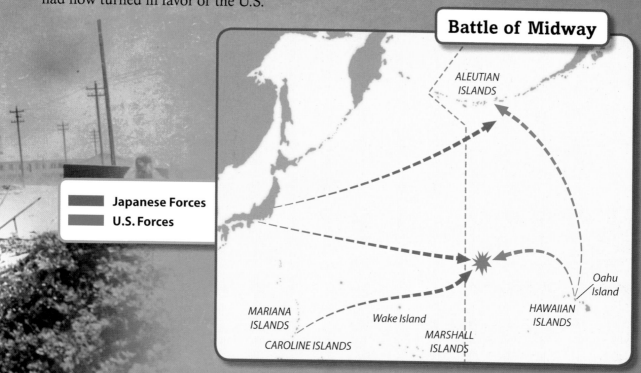

Battle of Midway

ALEUTIAN ISLANDS

Japanese Forces
U.S. Forces

MARIANA ISLANDS

Wake Island

MARSHALL ISLANDS

HAWAIIAN ISLANDS

Oahu Island

CAROLINE ISLANDS

John Basilone

In 1942, the Japanese were building a **strategic** airfield on the island of Guadalcanal in the Solomon Islands. From this airfield, the Japanese planned to launch bombers to destroy the vital supply lines linking the United States with its allies, Australia and New Zealand.

A Slow Start

On August 7, the Americans of the 1st Marine Division landed on Guadalcanal to try to put a stop to the Japanese plan. The Japanese didn't put up much of a fight at the start. However, once the Japanese regrouped, they battled back for many months.

John Basilone fought for the United States. Born in Buffalo, N.Y., but raised in New Jersey, Basilone first served with the U.S. Army in the Philippines. He later became a U.S. Marine machine gunner. On October 24, one **battalion** of Marines stood between the airfield and the enemy. Basilone commanded a unit of machine gunners in that battalion.

"It has been my ambition ever since Pearl Harbor to be with the outfit that recaptured Manila." —*John Basilone*

During the first assault on Guadalcanal, U.S. Marines took over Japanese strongholds.

John Basilone

Born:	November 4, 1916
Hometown:	Raritan, N.J.
Branch of Service:	U.S. Marines
Rank:	Sergeant
Heroic Moment:	Guadalcanal

Bullets in the Dark

The Marines had captured the airfield. As darkness fell, the Japanese launched a fierce frontal attack. With the fighting raging around him, Basilone tried to repair two damaged machine guns. He could not fix the first but managed to piece the second one together. Once he had finished, the enemy charged again. Using the rebuilt weapon, Basilone and his unit beat back the assault.

The battle dragged into the next day. Only Basilone and two of his men were left alive. Basilone ordered the men to keep two machine guns loaded at all times. He moved from one gun to another, firing each as he rolled to it. By 3 a.m., ammunition was running low. There were more bullets located some 100 yards away, in the line of enemy fire. To retrieve the shells, Basilone crawled through the jungle, dodging bullets.

The fighting was so fierce that Basilone had to leave cover a second time. This time the shells were 600 yards away. He dashed out, returning with ammo draped across his shoulders. When the fighting ended around daybreak, Basilone and his small band had beaten back the Japanese regiment.

The Guadalcanal Campaign continued until February 1943. At the island, American land forces established a much-needed foothold on the way to Japan. For his heroic actions at Guadalcanal and elsewhere, Basilone was awarded the **Congressional Medal of Honor**.

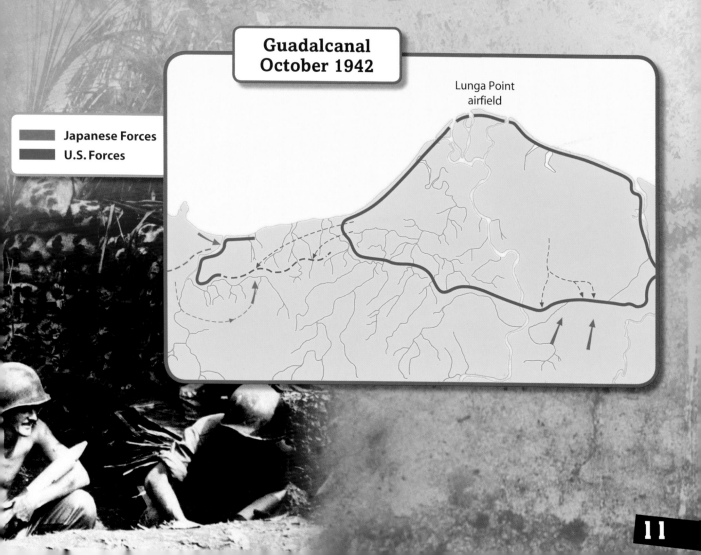

Guadalcanal October 1942

Lunga Point airfield

Japanese Forces
U.S. Forces

Georgi Zhukov

In 1939 and 1940, Nazi Germany stormed across Europe, conquering large parts of the continent. Germany's leader, Adolf Hitler, was poised to strike at the Soviet Union.

Friends No More

The two nations had been allies, but Hitler secretly had been using the alliance to buy time so his army could get ready to invade the Soviet Union. Germany crossed the border on June 22, 1941. Directing the Soviet defense was General Georgi Zhukov.

"If we come to a minefield, our infantry attacks exactly as it were not there."
—*Georgi Zhukov* (on right)

When Germany violated a non-aggression pact in 1941, Josef Stalin joined the Allies.

Defending Stalin's City

Zhukov was outspoken, stern, and often at odds with Soviet leader Josef Stalin. Yet, in August 1942, Stalin appointed Zhukov his deputy supreme commander. The general was directed to defend Stalingrad, in southwestern Russia, at any cost.

Stalingrad, today called Volgograd, was a strategic city on the Volga River. It had many factories. It was also the gateway to the oil-rich Caucasus region. By capturing Stalingrad, the Nazis hoped to obtain the oil needed to keep their war machine running. By August 23, 1942, the Germans had reached the Volga. German artillery, tanks, and planes pounded Stalingrad into rubble.

Georgi Zhukov

Born:	December 1, 1896
Hometown:	Strelkovka, Russia
Branch of Service:	Soviet Army
Rank:	General
Heroic Moment:	Battle of Stalingrad

Nazis on the Move

By September, the Germans had taken several strategic hills overlooking the city. **Infantry** and tanks then stormed into Stalingrad. Zhukov formed a line of defense, hoping to wear down the Nazis. Once the Germans had weakened, he planned to launch a **counterattack**. Zhukov moved supplies, ammunition, and soldiers east of Stalingrad, ready to strike at the proper moment.

Retreat Denied

Stalingrad's narrow, rubble-strewn streets slowed the Nazis. The harsh Russian winter hurt the Germans, too. They did not have proper clothing or enough food. On November 19, Zhukov ordered the Soviet reserve units into battle. The charge caught the Nazis by surprise. Germany's Sixth Army was nearly surrounded. Nazi leaders pleaded with Hitler to allow the troops to retreat. Hitler refused. He promised **reinforcements** and supplies, which never arrived.

Bloodiest Battle

The Germans surrendered on February 2, 1943. Stalingrad was the bloodiest battle of the war. There were about 2 million total casualties. It was the first real German defeat in Europe. Zhukov went on to rout Hitler's armies at the Battle of Kursk in 1943. The Soviet general also led the final assault on Berlin in 1945.

The firing on Stalingrad was relentless.

George S. Patton

General George Patton was always on the move, swiftly cutting across the battlefield. His nickname during World War II was Old Blood and Guts, or as his soldiers joked, "Our blood and his guts."

The General Who Roared

A graduate of the U.S. Military Academy at West Point, Patton came from a long line of military men. Several, including his grandfather, fought in the U.S. Civil War (1861–1865). Patton was often gruff and almost never diplomatic. Patton's bosses were often critical of him.

"Accept the challenges so that you can feel the exhilaration of victory."
—*George S. Patton*

Defeat at Kasserine

In November 1942, Britain and the United States invaded North Africa. At that point, the Americans were new to combat, and that winter brought one of the greatest U.S. defeats. In February 1943, the Germans overwhelmed the Americans at the Kasserine Pass in Tunisia. Many U.S. soldiers panicked and fled. There were 6,500 U.S. casualties.

George S. Patton

Born:	November 11, 1885
Hometown:	San Gabriel, California
Branch of Service:	U.S. Army
Rank:	General
Heroic Moment:	North African and Sicilian Campaigns

U.S. forces moved into North Africa with heavy equipment.

Patton Takes Charge

After the Kasserine disaster, General Dwight D. Eisenhower placed Patton in command. Patton was a master of tank warfare. He whipped his men into shape. By March, Patton counterattacked and helped push the Germans out of Africa.

U.S. artillery units took positions in the hills in Sicily.

Sicily in the Crosshairs

Patton's superiors then put the general in charge of the U.S. Seventh Army. Patton's mission was to march the Americans across western Sicily (a strategic Italian island) and then drive east toward Messina. From Messina, the Allies could more easily invade the Italian mainland. However, British Field Marshal Bernard Montgomery also expected to lead the Allied forces. Allied commanders gave Montgomery permission to drive straight into the city. The plan made Patton angry.

A Horse Race

On July 10, 1943, Patton's army left North Africa and landed on the beaches along Sicily's southwest coast. Montgomery and his men went ashore to the east of the Americans. Patton was not about to let the British take Messina first. Patton moved fast. "This is a horse race, in which the prestige of the U.S. Army is at stake," he wrote to one of his commanders. On August 17, 1943, Patton arrived in Messina hours ahead of the British. The capture of Sicily paved the way for the invasion of Southern Europe.

Tommy Macpherson

Days before the Allies invaded Normandy, France, in June 1944, British Prime Minister Winston Churchill told Major Tommy Macpherson to wreak havoc on the Nazis and to "set Europe ablaze."

Officer in a Kilt

Macpherson was no ordinary soldier. He was a **commando**. His mission was to carry out secret raids deep within enemy territory. Macpherson parachuted behind enemy lines on June 8, 1944, two days after D-Day. Macpherson's job was to arm and train members of the French Resistance, a group of brave civilians who fought against the Nazis.

The *Ordre National de la Légion d'Honneur*, or National Order of the Legion of Honor, is the highest honor in France. Macpherson was given the highest rank within the order, that of a knight, or Chevalier.

British soldiers waited for the signal to move forward after landing at Normandy. Tommy Macpherson parachuted inland.

Tommy Macpherson

Born:	October 4, 1920
Hometown:	Edinburgh, Scotland
Branch of Service:	British Army
Rank:	Major
Heroic Moment:	Invasion of Europe, other events

Hit and Run

With no time to waste, Macpherson's group blocked the road with fallen trees and hid their only anti-tank **mine**. The Germans stopped to remove the trees. One of their tanks hit the mine and blew up. Macpherson and his band hid in the woods, gunning down as many Germans as they could. Macpherson and the Resistance fighters then escaped from the scene of the fighting.

Hours later, the convoy began moving again. Macpherson followed, constantly firing and running away. These hit-and-run **tactics** slowed the German column to a crawl. It should have taken the tanks three days to reach Normandy. Instead it took two weeks. By that time, the Allies had secured the beaches.

The French Resistance fought in concert with the British to help sabotage the Germans.

A Military Legend

Macpherson became a legend. He blew up electrical towers and bridges. He was so successful that the Nazis offered a 300,000-franc reward for his capture. In one incident, the Germans outgunned and outmanned Macpherson and his troops. Yet he convinced the German general into surrendering. Macpherson's courage and daring made him the most decorated soldier in British history.

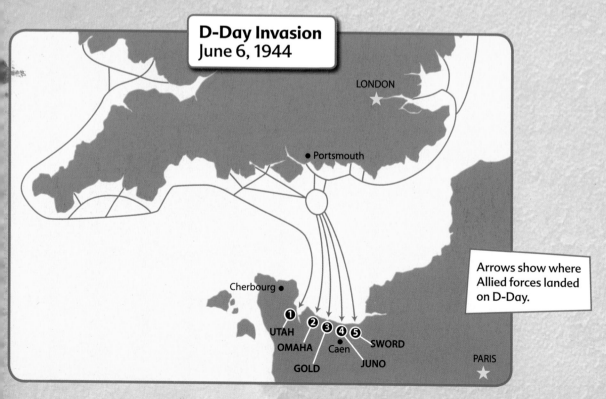

D-Day Invasion
June 6, 1944

LONDON

• Portsmouth

Arrows show where Allied forces landed on D-Day.

Cherbourg •

① UTAH
② ③ ④ ⑤
OMAHA   Caen   SWORD
         JUNO
GOLD

PARIS

Audie Murphy

Audie Murphy became the most decorated soldier in U.S. history. He won 33 U.S. citations and awards, including the Medal of Honor.

Last Foothold in France

Murphy, the son of Texas sharecroppers, joined the Army when he was a teenager. In 1945, Murphy was serving as a second lieutenant in the 3rd Infantry Division. He was commander of Company B, which was in the advance on Berlin. In January, Murphy and the men of Company B found themselves in a dangerous position. They were outside the French town of Holtzwihr, near the German border. The Germans were determined to take the area back and keep one of their last footholds in France.

"Lead from the front." —*Audie Murphy*

Audie Murphy

Born:	June 20, 1924
Hometown:	Kingston, Texas, vicinity
Branch of Service:	U.S. Army
Rank:	Second Lieutenant
Heroic Moment:	European Campaign

U.S. fighters fought in snow in Belgium in January 1945.

Army of One

The Nazis opened fire, killing or wounding 102 men of Company B. All the officers were dead—except Murphy. As six German tanks and 250 troops moved forward, Murphy ordered his men to safer ground. Murphy stood alone and battled the oncoming Germans. Despite heavy fire, Murphy stayed at his position. Using a field telephone, he guided the artillery, telling gunners where to aim.

U.S. infantry streamed over the French countryside in 1945, making their way to the German border.

Nazis Advance

Murphy climbed aboard a burning tank destroyer as the German tanks closed in. He trained the vehicle's machine gun on the advancing Nazis. Surrounded on three sides, Murphy killed dozens of German troops. The German tanks withdrew. For yet another hour the enemy tried to kill Murphy. He held his position.

Wounded but Fighting

At one point, a Nazi bullet hit Murphy in the leg, but he kept firing. When his ammunition ran out, Murphy finally made his way back to the rest of the company. Refusing medical attention, he coordinated a counterattack, forcing the Germans to retreat. Murphy's heroics on January 26, 1945, saved many Allied lives. His brave actions allowed the Allies to control the woods around Holtzwihr. The Germans eventually left France, never to return.

Anthony McAuliffe

General Anthony McAuliffe was ordered to protect Bastogne at all costs.

Splitting the Allies

In December 1944, the Allies were squeezing Hitler's armies. The Russians marched from the east, and the Americans and British moved from the west. Hitler launched a **counteroffensive** on the British and Americans in Belgium. German tanks and infantry were sent through the heavily wooded, snow-covered Ardennes Forest in order to split the Allied forces. The Nazis planned to capture the Belgian port city of Antwerp.

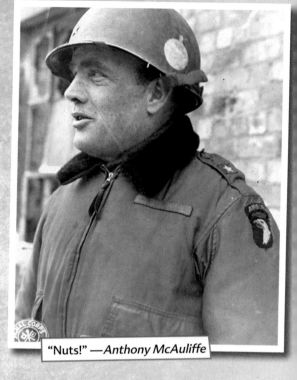

"Nuts!" —Anthony McAuliffe

Battle of the Bulge

The Allied front stretched from southern Belgium into Luxembourg. About 250,000 German troops attacked on December 16, 1944. Despite snow, ice, and wind, German forces advanced 50 miles into the Allied frontline. That created a dangerous "bulge" in the Allied line of defense.

The Germans reached Bastogne, a small Belgian town protected by the 101st Airborne Division. Bastogne was important because a network of roads stretched westward from there. The Germans surrounded the town and the U.S. soldiers, under the command of Anthony McAuliffe.

Anthony McAuliffe

Born:	July 2, 1898
Hometown:	Washington, D.C.
Branch of Service:	U.S. Army
Rank:	General
Heroic Moment:	Siege of Bastogne

The soldiers who fought in the frozen Belgian forest were not allowed to build fires, so they dug trenches to try to stay warm.

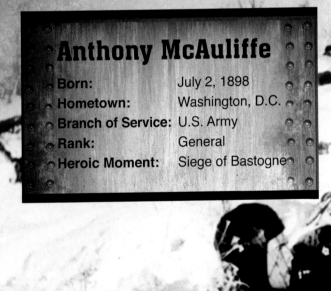

Under Fire

It was not an easy assignment. The brutal winter weather and the constant shelling by the Germans put the soldiers of the 101st in a nearly hopeless situation. Medicine was in short supply, as were ammunition and food. Bad weather kept Allied planes from arriving with supplies.

NUTS!

On December 22, four Germans walked up the road with a white flag. The Germans were also carrying a written demand that the Allies surrender. McAuliffe, a West Point graduate who had jumped from a plane on D-Day, replied by writing, "NUTS!" A U.S. officer had to explain to the Germans that this meant no… and never.

Rescued

The next morning, the sun came out. Soon, the sky filled with American cargo planes, which dropped medical supplies, food, blankets, and ammunition. U.S. General George Patton's tanks swooped in next. The **siege** of Bastogne ended, and the Allies later won the Battle of the Bulge. The Germans would never mount a major offensive in Europe again.

Much-needed supplies were dropped to soldiers caught in Bastogne in December 1944.

Henry Mucci

Lieutenant Colonel Henry Mucci, a West Point graduate and U.S. Army Ranger, was assigned to rescue the survivors at a prison camp in the Philippines.

Bataan Death March

The Japanese captured 70,000 to 100,000 prisoners of war (POWs) in April 1942. They then forced most of the prisoners to march from Bataan, on the island of Luzon, to a prison camp near Cabanatuan. Many Allied troops on the Bataan Death March, which included 63 miles of walking, died of exhaustion, disease, and starvation. The Japanese brutally killed many more.

Returning to Fight

Americans returned to the Philippines two years later. Filipino scouts told them that the Japanese were planning to murder or move the Cabanatuan prisoners. Many of the POWs had already died of disease and starvation. Out of the 54,000 original U.S. and Filipino POWs, only 511 had survived.

"I only want men who feel lucky."
—Henry Mucci

Henry Mucci

Born:	March 4, 1911
Hometown:	Bridgeport, Connecticut
Branch of Service:	U.S. Army
Rank:	Lieutenant Colonel
Heroic Moment:	Cabanatuan Prison Raid

On the Bataan Death March, those who were weakened by hunger or thirst were carried.

Surprise, Surprise!

Mucci decided to march his men 30 miles behind enemy lines and launch a surprise attack on Cabanatuan. Hundreds of Filipino **guerrillas** joined in the assault. Their job was to prevent Japanese reinforcements from launching a counterattack.

Prison Camp Raid

Mucci began his mission on January 28, 1945. By nightfall, Mucci's force was in enemy territory. The Filipino guerrillas arranged for dozens of carts to move the POWs who might be too weak to walk.

As the sun set on January 30, Mucci's men positioned themselves for the attack. That night, the Americans fired on the Japanese with overwhelming force. The Americans destroyed guard towers and the **pillboxes** that housed Japanese machine gun teams. At the same time, the Filipino guerrillas stopped the Japanese from launching a counterstrike across a bridge a few miles away.

The Allies took war prisoners as well. At Okinawa, the Japanese prisoners were held behind barbed wire.

Success

The raid was over in about 15 minutes. Mucci and his men rescued all but one of the prisoners. The U.S. Rangers killed more than 500 Japanese soldiers. Only two Rangers died in the assault. The military awarded Mucci the Distinguished Service Cross.

Daniel Inouye

Daniel Inouye was 17 years old on September 7, 1941. He was dressing at his home on Coyne Street in Honolulu when he heard a radio news flash that the Japanese were attacking Pearl Harbor.

Helping the Wounded

Inouye, the son of Japanese immigrants, ran outside and saw the dark smoke of burning ships and buildings in the distance. The phone rang. The secretary of the local Red Cross was on the line. He asked Inouye, a first-aid instructor, to come help the wounded. Inouye didn't return home for five days.

442nd Regimental Combat Team

A few months later, the U.S. government placed thousands of Japanese Americans on the West Coast in **internment** camps. The government feared Japanese Americans would be loyal to Japan. That was not the case. Eventually the government allowed Inouye and others to enlist in the Army. The Japanese Americans formed the 442nd Regimental Combat Team. The 442nd would become the most highly decorated unit in the U.S. Army. Inouye quickly became a sergeant and a **platoon** leader. He went to Italy in 1944 and then fought in France.

"One doesn't become a soldier in a week." —*Daniel Inouye*

Daniel Inouye witnessed the attack on Pearl Harbor from his home.

Daniel Inouye

Born:	September 7, 1924
Hometown:	Honolulu, Hawaii
Branch of Service:	U.S. Army
Rank:	Second Lieutenant
Heroic Moment:	Colle Musatello, Italy

Colle Musatello

On April 21, 1945, Inouye was back in Italy as a second lieutenant. He was ordered to capture a rocky ridge called Colle Musatello in northeast Italy. The order was part of a larger campaign to push the Germans out of Italy's Po Valley.

When three German machine guns opened fire, Inouye grabbed a grenade and moved toward the nearest machine gun nest. A German bullet pierced his stomach. Inouye still ran forward. He tossed the grenade into the bunker and shot the dazed German machine gun crew as they stumbled out of their lair.

Never Say Die

Inouye staggered up the hill once more and silenced a second machine gun nest. As he raised his arm to toss another grenade, a German soldier shot him, nearly tearing his arm off. Inouye somehow threw the live grenade and kept firing. The Americans won the Po Valley campaign, forcing the Germans to surrender in Italy. Inouye recovered from his wounds and later became a U.S. senator.

In April 1945, Allied troops climbed the Tuscan Apennines, between the Po Valley and the Italian lands of Tuscany and Lazio.

Hall of Heroes

Some heroes of World War II became famous; others were lost to history. Here are some of the people who went beyond the call of duty.

John F. Kennedy

On August 1, 1943, John F. Kennedy was in command of PT 109, a U.S. Navy torpedo boat on patrol in the Solomon Islands. In the night, a Japanese destroyer rammed the boat, forcing the crew into the sea. Kennedy ordered the survivors to swim to a nearby island. He towed one of the wounded sailors by the strap on the sailor's life vest. Kennedy later found two island scouts who worked for the Allies. He carved a message on a coconut and gave it to them, which led to a rescue. In 1961, the former PT commander became President Kennedy, the 35th U.S. president. He placed the coconut on his desk at the White House.

John F. Kennedy was 26 at the time of the PT-109 incident.

Navajo Code Talkers

Because the Japanese were good at breaking secret U.S. military codes, the Marines started sending messages in Navajo, a Native American language. Only a few people outside the Navajo nation knew how to speak it. Although the Japanese could hear the messages, they could not crack the code. The Navajos who sent and translated the messages were known as code talkers. They helped win many battles in the Pacific.

The role of the code breakers was kept secret until 1968.

Tuskegee Airmen

The Tuskegee Airmen were America's first African American military pilots. They were dedicated to the country's defense and to making history for African Americans. The pilots trained to fly fighter planes at the Tuskegee Army Air Field in Tuskegee, Alabama. They formed the 99th Fighter Squadron. During the war in Europe and North Africa, the airmen flew 15,533 missions. They shot down 111 German aircraft and destroyed more than 120 on the ground. In 2007, the 300 surviving Tuskegee Airmen received the Congressional Gold Medal.

None of the bombers escorted by the Tuskegee Airmen was lost to enemy fire.

General Theodore Roosevelt, Jr.

Theodore Roosevelt, Jr., had served in World War I. By the time of World War II, he was not in the best of health. Despite arthritis, he landed with Allied troops in France on D-Day. The son of President Theodore Roosevelt was the first general to hit the beaches. However, he and his men landed at the wrong spot. "We'll start the war from right here," he told them. Roosevelt led several assaults along the beachhead, defeating the Nazis at each stop. He died five weeks later of a heart attack. He received the Medal of Honor posthumously.

Women Airforce Service Pilots

Because the war created a shortage of pilots in the United States, the U.S. Army recruited females to join the Women Airforce Service Pilots, or WASPs. More than 1,000 women ferried supplies, bombs, and planes across the United States. The Army paid each WASP just $250 a month, with no benefits. Yet the WASPs flew 60 million miles.

The women of the WASPs came from every socioeconomic background.

Heroes of the Holocaust

As the war in Europe was ending in 1945, the Allies liberated the prisoners in the Nazi death camps. The Germans had built the concentration camps as part of Hitler's "Final Solution," his plan to extinguish the Jewish people and other groups.

Many Jews fled Europe when Hitler first came to power, but millions did not. As the Nazis marched into new countries, they imprisoned the Jews in concentration camps, such as Bergen-Belsen, Buchenwald, Auschwitz, Treblinka, and Dachau. Eventually some of the concentration camps were converted into death camps, where the Nazis murdered millions of Jews and others whom the Nazis thought to be inferior.

At the war's end, some children made it out of the camp in Lambach, Austria, alive.

Holocaust

The Germans forced many people in the camps to work as slave laborers. They used others for "scientific research." Historians call this organized, state-sponsored murder of the Jews, the Holocaust. By the end of the war, the Nazis had slaughtered 6 million people. However, during the war years, many people risked their lives to help thousands of Jews escape the Nazis. These are the few of their stories.

Irena Sendler

Irena Sendler was born just outside Warsaw, Poland, in 1910. Starting in 1939, the Nazis herded hundreds of thousands of Jews into a tiny ghetto in Warsaw. Thousands of the Jews died there of disease and starvation.

The Germans allowed Sendler, a non-Jew, into the ghetto. At first she brought food and medicine. She then created a system to sneak the children out of the ghetto. One man smuggled a baby out by putting the child inside his toolbox. Other children were hidden in body bags. Sendler provided the children with fake papers. She found them homes in private residences, orphanages, and convents. She saved approximately 2,500 children. Sendler buried a jar with the names of the children. She hoped to one day reunite the children with their families.

Irena Sendler's code name was Jolanta.

In 1943, the Nazis escorted Jews from the ghetto in Warsaw to the camps.

Oskar Schindler

Oskar Schindler began the war as the most unlikely of heroes. He was a brash businessman who supplied the German army with supplies. He made friends with Nazi officers and made a great deal of money. As he did so, however, Schindler shielded Jews from the Nazis. Many Jews worked at his Krakow, Poland, factory. He called them "essential" employees and bribed Nazi officials to allow the Jews to stay. In 1944, the Soviet Army closed in on Krakow. Schindler persuaded the Nazis to open an ammunition factory in Moravia. One of Schindler's assistants listed nearly 1,200 Jewish prisoners that Schindler insisted he needed for the new factory.

Oskar Schindler (seated) was later thanked by the people he had saved. A famous movie, *Schindler's List*, was made about him.

Raoul Wallenberg

Raoul Wallenberg was a Swedish diplomat who rescued thousands of Jews in Budapest, Hungary. Although Hungary was originally in alliance with Nazi Germany, a number of defeats led the Hungarian government to seek an **armistice** with the Allies. In retaliation, the Nazis set up a pro-German government in Hungary. The government's leaders sent thousands of Hungarian Jews to Nazi camps in Poland. By July 1944, about 440,000 Jews had been removed from Hungary.

With the backing of the Swedish government, Wallenberg issued "certificates of protection" to the Jews in Budapest. Those official papers spared thousands of Jews from the concentration camps. In addition, he helped establish hospitals, nurseries, and a soup kitchen. When the Soviet Army arrived in Budapest in 1945, some 100,000 Jews were still alive—thanks to Raoul Wallenberg and others.

Raoul Wallenberg issued certificates of protection under the authority of the Swedish government.

Nicholas Winton

Nicholas Winton was a young British stockbroker when he visited Prague, Czechoslovakia, in 1938. While in Prague, Winton was surprised at the number of Jewish refugees streaming into the city. They were fleeing a Nazi invasion. Winton decided to help the children get out of the country. He established an organization that arranged for trains to transport the children to Great Britain. He advertised in England in order to find placements for each child. Winton provided safe passage for 669 children from Czechoslovakia before World War II broke out.

Nicholas Winton was eventually knighted by the Queen of England.

Varian Fry

In June 1940, Germany invaded France. At the time, an American relief organization sent journalist Varian Fry to France to aid those who might feel the wrath of the Nazis. Fry set up a network of people in France and elsewhere who gave him forged documents that he passed on to those in danger. Fry's network also created secret escape routes. For 13 months, Fry risked his own life and freedom to help 2,000 people escape the Nazis, including many noted artists, scientists, and authors.

Among the people Varian Fry saved were the artists Marc Chagall and Max Ernst.

Glossary

armistice—a temporary truce between opponents before the signing of a treaty

aviator—an airplane pilot

battalion—a military unit; U.S. battalions have three or more companies

commando—a soldier trained and organized for surprise raids in enemy territory

Congressional Medal of Honor—the highest U.S. military honor a soldier can receive

counterattack—an attack made in response to an enemy's attack

counteroffensive—a large-scale counterattack

court-martial—a military court for members of the armed forces; or to try a case in such a court

guerrillas—soldiers who engage in irregular warfare, especially as members of an independent unit

infantry—soldiers who are trained to fight on foot

internment—imprisonment; confinement

mine—an explosive device placed in the ground or under water

pillboxes—small concrete structures that house machine guns

platoon—a military unit that is a subdivision of a company

reinforcements—troops that strengthen or come to the aid of a military force

siege—a military blockade of a fortified place

strategic—required to conduct warfare effectively; essential to planning

tactics—a planned action or maneuver during combat

Index

Basilone, John   10, 11

Doolittle, James H.   6–8

Fry, Varian   31

Inouye, Daniel   24, 25

Kennedy, John F.   26

Macpherson, Tommy   16, 17

McAuliffe, Anthony   20, 21

Mucci, Henry   22, 23

Murphy, Audie   18, 19

Navajo code talkers   26

Nimitz, Chester W.   8, 9

Patton, George S.   14, 15, 21

Roosevelt, General Theodore, Jr.   27

Schindler, Oskar   30

Sendler, Irena   29

Tuskegee Airmen   27

Wallenberg, Raoul   30

Winton, Nicholas   31

Women Airforce Service Pilots (WASPs)   27

Zhukov, Georgi   12, 13